D0688177

PLEASE CHECK FOR 4 CDs in front
BEFORE AND AFTER EACH CIRCULATION

La Danse

DAVID HAMILTON

ISBN 3-937406-18-2

Design by Torsten Jahnke, mitchum d.a.
Produced by optimal media production GmbH, Röbel/Germany
Printed and manufactured in Germany

EarBooks is a division of edel CLASSICS GmbH
For more information about EarBooks please visit www.earbooks.net

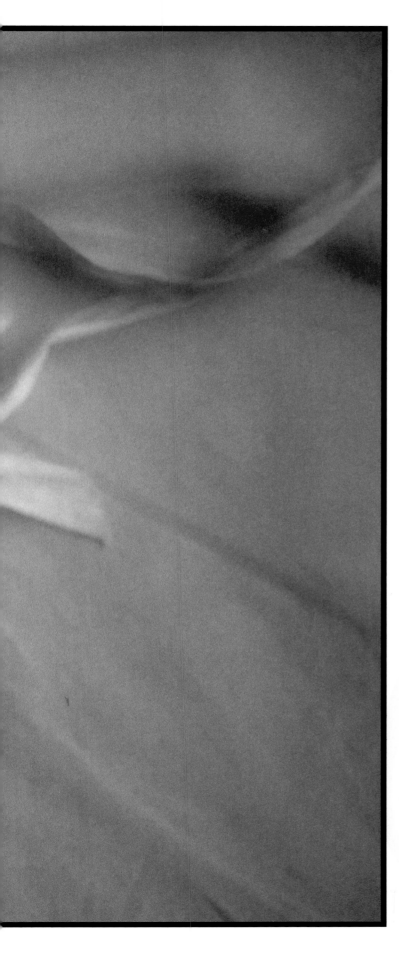

The Ballet

Music – pliant or concrete.
Decor – elaborate or simple.
Above all else the body trained to express
the complete range of human involvement.
For us, the audience,
it is communication by beauty
identification with stylised movement
transmission of antagonisms.

~

Day by day, life may lack
happiness
freedom
involvement
identification.

~

This can be found in THE DANCE.
It is a living Art.

~

Arresting magnetism draws the eye
to the simplicity, yet complexity of the line.
The excitement of space-spanning leaps
the thrill of perfect control
the stillness of strength in repose
the interrelation of body and body
the mystic beauty of the light
the formality or informality of costume and decor.

~

Such is BALLET.

~

Dancers start with themselves.
They present humanity in all its facets.
The onlookers will make of it what they will,
but the dancers are true to themselves.

~

They offer.

~

We accept.

The Barre

In a fantasy dream world
of beamed attic rehearsal rooms,
opening onto rooftops and scented
with the mustiness of costumes and rosin
the bareness is brought alive to be peopled
with the reality of relationships,
yet always disciplined –
by THE BARRE.

Precision
promises the vast embrace of thought
the infinite capacity
for LOVE
directness
emotion.

Perfection is the accident of birth
coupled with the vigorous discipline of training.

SONIA PETROVA

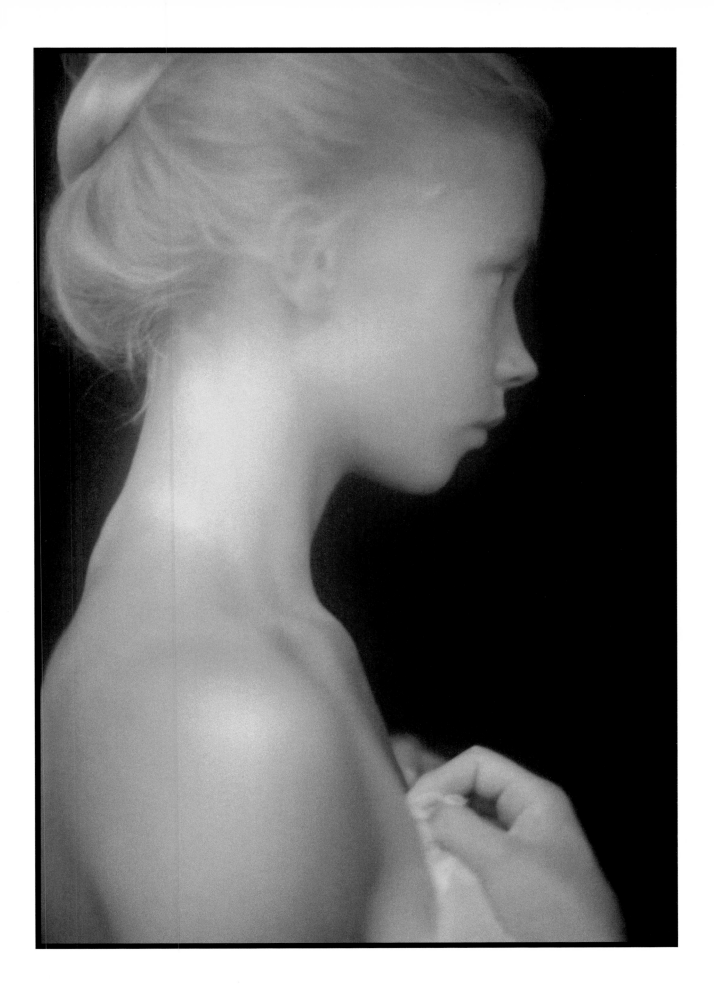

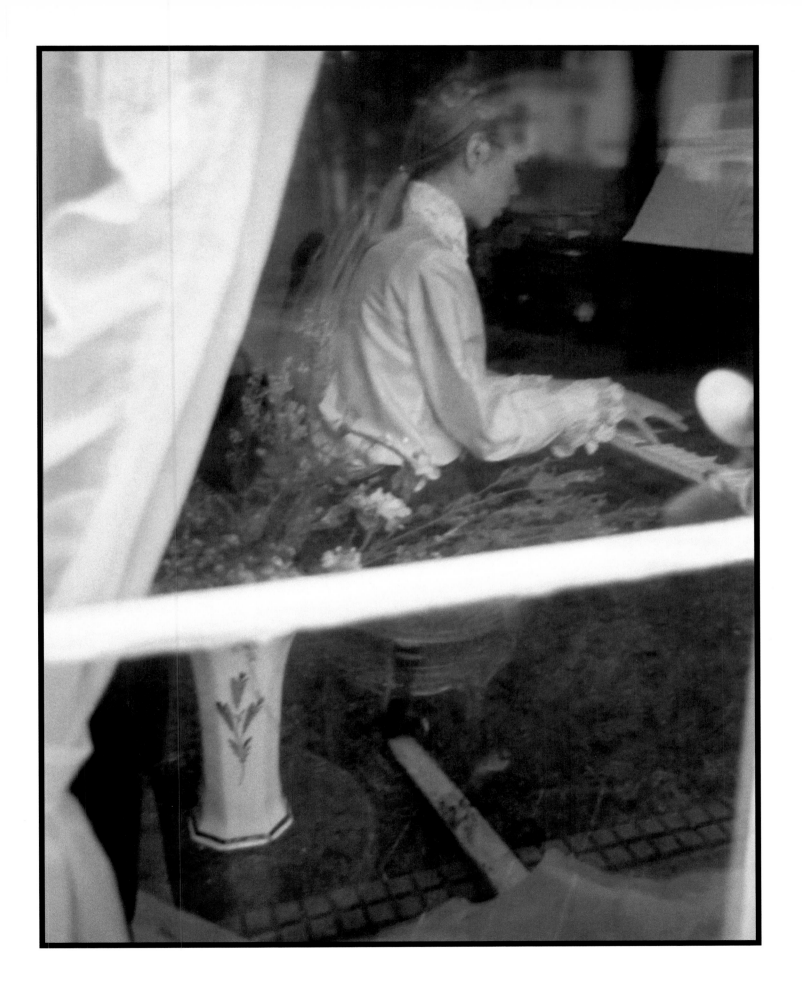

SUZANNE FARELL

Accomplishment in Dance

Here is a torch –
THE DANCE has caught alight –
not for one troupe,
for one nation only:
around the world the flame
spreads blazing excitement,
urging towards greatness
dancers who before were lacking in fire.
Challenge provokes dancers'
aspirations in art.
Creative talents heap works on their shoulders.
Musicians rise to meet demanding standards,
costumes and great sets embellish the scene –
here is THE TORCH.

Rudolf Nureyev

From dreams when young have come
his famed achievements.

»*Choreography, like love,*
is done in pairs.«

BÉJART

ROBERT DENVERS

RITA POELVOORDE

Pas de deux

After all the rigours of discipline and training,
it is the PAS DE DEUX that holds the greatest delight
both for dancers and the audience.
The bravura exhibitionism of a solo,
the awe-inspiring uniformity of a corps de ballet,
each has its place,
but loneliness and regimentation
are two problems of our time.

~

The interrelationship of a couple in the PAS DE DEUX
can be transmitted across the footlights with out losing its intimacy -
and speak of love and despair, of hope and joy.
The meeting of eyes, the opening heart,
the carefree leap, the exciting turn and the flight to fancy,
all are within its compass.

Vitality and movement spring from the feet;
they are the fundament of all ballet expression;
they speak a language of their own.

With arms and legs and
perfect grace
and swirls
and twirls
and moving face:
Enchantress weave your spell.
~
The soft concern of heart and eye
conceals from him
that he will die
if out of heaven,
he opts for hell.
But hell is not within these arms,
nor is it hell
to have such charms for daily bread.

'Tis nothing save a raucous bout
of jealous heart and gall.

~

Thus is the battle fought and won,
she wants him with her in the sun.

~

Woman is All

~

Far on the distant shores he hears a murmur
faint from earlier years:

~

The Dance is All

~

Who now can tell the truth of this
for him – both dance and love were bliss.

~

Yet each did take its toll.

Children to the Dance

Where does it all begin?
With the body.
What motivates?
The desire for fuller expression
not limited to words.

~

It starts early,
for the limbs have to be formed
to encompass a vocabulary.
It extends from one
to two and eventually involves a whole company,
then the entire world.
Work, dedication,
the self-consuming passion of perfection.

~

It is not for those who treat it as a social accomplishment.
For those filled with the spirit of the true dance,
it is a lifetime of giving.

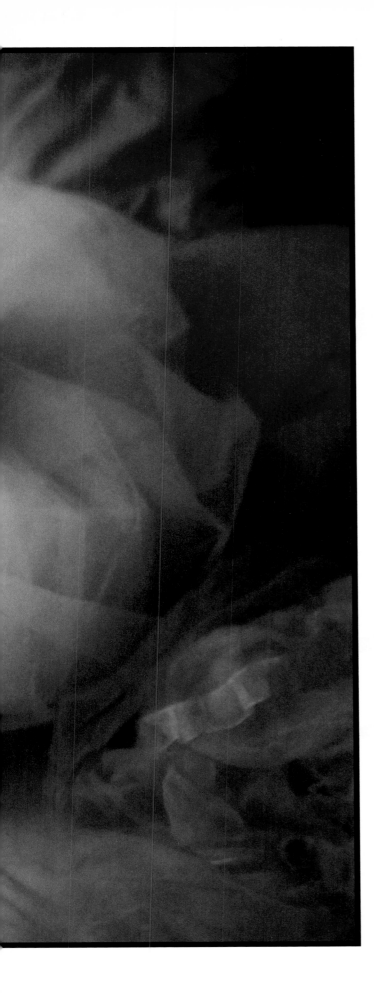

The desire consumes.
There is no satisfactory substitute;
once felt, the only release is to perform.
~

Inspired by the legend of Karsavina or Nijinsky,
Fonteyn or Nureyev,
the child must dance.
~

And school's rigorous discipline
is happily endured to that great end:
the first performance.

Young Dancers

From each, an evocation of beauty
timeless, yet alive.
Dark, fair; short, tall.
Faces – etched round deep pools of eyes and mouths,
like the surface of water rippled by the breeze
with sun shining on it –
the flashed communication of an eye.

~

The bloom of face
pointed by the arc of an eyebrow.
Tresses floating, long, luxurious,
controlled – abandoned.
Curved neck and arm relaxed,
poised – delineating.

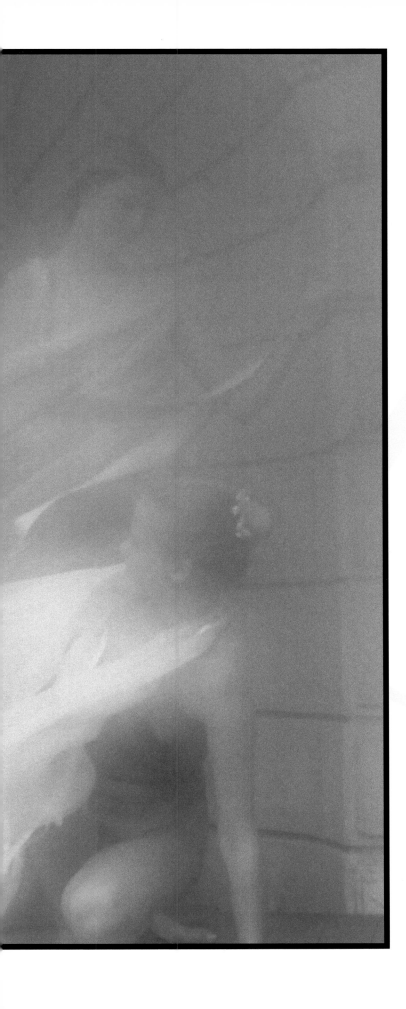

These creatures, it seems,

are the substance of dreams.

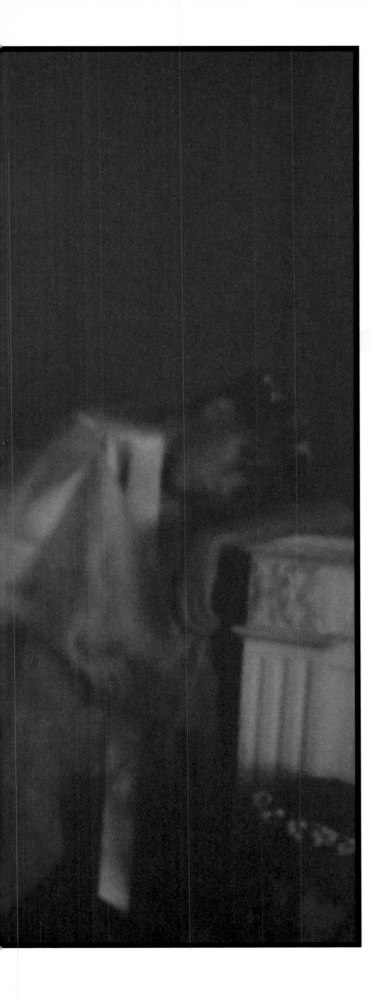

»True ease in writing
comes from art not chance,
as those move easiest
who have learned to dance.«

ALEXANDER POPE

On stage art conceals art to reveal

the appearance of effortless expression.

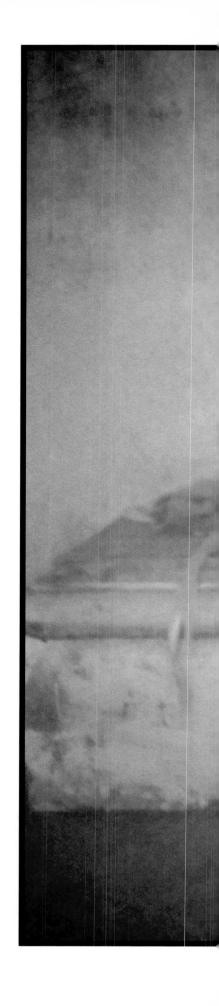

»It is peoples' movement that consoles us.
If the leaves of a tree did not move,
how sad would be the tree – and so should we.«

EDGAR DEGAS

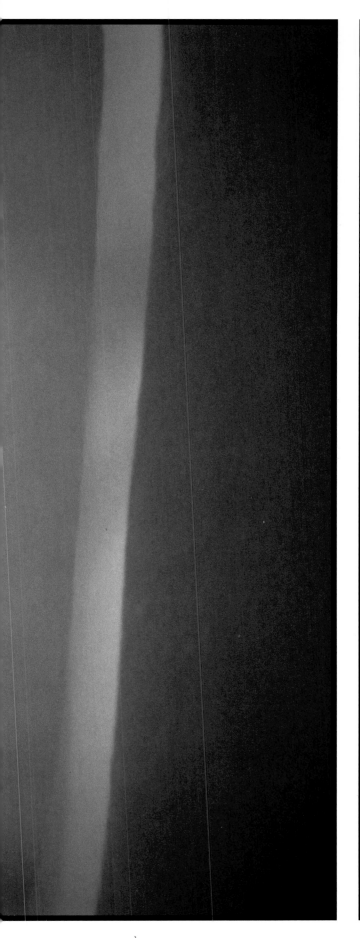

The Dance

No one doubts the dawn.
It is the expectation of a new day
promising
sun
rain
soft and warm breezes
hard and clear light
fierceness
joy
sound
speech
and movement.
~
So too THE DANCE,
A capacity through stillness or movement
to speak
relax
involve
enchant
seduce
terrify
antagonise
uplift,
but above all else
INVOLVE.

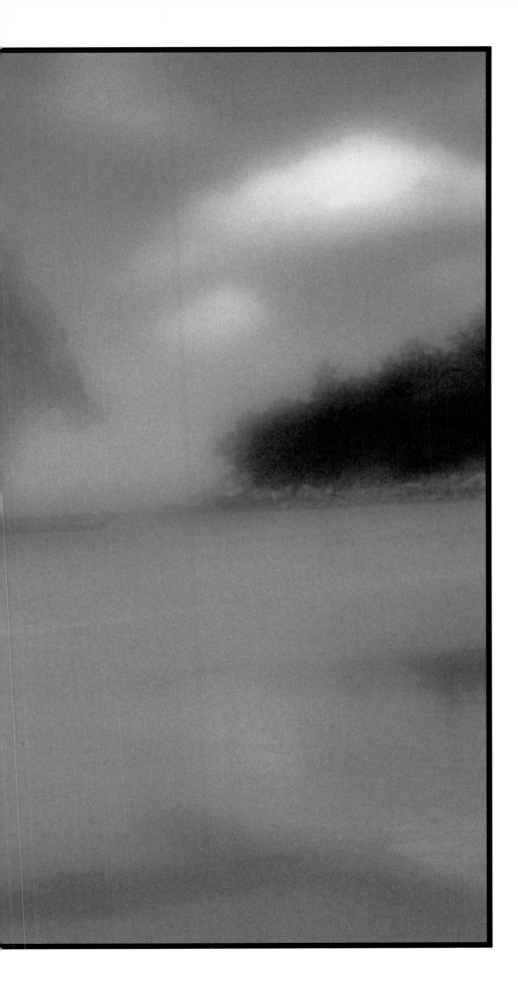

Arms embrace thought?
Legs support the whole of reason?
The body is the soul?
Still or in flight, on stage or off,
you are inheritors of spirits
you wield power to captivate
and tell a story;
appal, excite, enthral
in what you do.
~
Modern or classic
facets of the same powerful force –
and you claim silence as your right,
to weave a magic spell of art
which speaks directly to my haunted heart.
Still haunted by questions
of THE DANCE.

Dance across the World

London, Brussels, New York,
Leningrad, Naples,
Zurich, Rome, Copenhagen, Paris,
Catania, Biarritz, Amsterdan,
Milan, Barcelona,
Spoleto.

~

Dance is international speech,
an embassy of peace.

~

They dance across the world,
they speak in gestures
to the secret places of the soul.
Joy is founded in a true beauty of form.

Tracklisting

CD I

PETER ILYICH TCHAIKOVSKY
(1840–1893)

La Belle au Bois Dormant
Sleeping Beauty, Op. 66
(Highlights)

1	*Introduction*	3:15
2	*No. 1 Marche (March)*	4:44
3	*No. 2 Scène dansante*	4:37
4	*No. 3 Pas de six*	11:22
	Introduction - Adagio	
	Variations I–VI and Coda	
5	*No. 6 Valse (Waltz)*	4:54
6	*No. 10 Entr'acte et scène*	2:50
7	*No. 14 Scène*	5:34
8	*No. 15a Pas d'action*	6:22
9	*No. 23 Pas de quatre*	3:27
	Variations II and IV	
	Coda	
10	*No. 30 Finale*	6:23

Rundfunk-Sinfonie-Orchester Berlin
Heinz Rögner

(P) 1981*

CD II

PETER ILYICH TCHAIKOVSKY
(1840–1893)

Le Lac des Cygnes
Swan Lake, Op. 20
(Highlights)

1	*Introduction*	3:01
2	*No. 2 Vales (Waltz)*	5:57
3	*No. 5 Pas de deux (Duet)*	10:06
4	*No. 13 Danse des petits cygnes* *(Dance of the little swans)*	11:22
5	*No. 14 Scène*	2:48
6	*No. 20 Danse hongroise* *(Hungarian dance)*	3:25
7	*No. 21 Danse espagnole* *(Spanish dance)*	2:42
8	*No. 22 Danse neapolitaine* *(Neapolitan dance)*	1:45
9	*No. 23 Mazurka (Polish dance)*	4:07
10	*No. 28 Scène*	4:19
11	*No. 29 Finale*	4:41

Rundfunk-Sinfonie-Orchester Berlin
Heinz Rögner

(P) 1981*

CD III

CLAUDE DEBUSSY
(1862–1918)

1	*Prélude à l'après-midi d'un Faune*	9:27
	(Prelude to the Afternoon of a Faun)	

Fritz Rucker, flute
Staatskapelle Dresden
Otmar Suitner

(P) 1969*

FELIX MENDELSSOHN BARTHOLDY
(1809–1847)

A Midsummer Night's Dream, Op. 61

2	*Overture*	11:53
3	*Allegro vivace*	1:14

Staatskapelle Berlin
Günther Herbig

(P) 1977*

FRANZ SCHUBERT (1797–1828)
Rosamunde, Op. 26 D. 797

4	*Ballet Music No. 1*	7:22

Staatskapelle Dresden
Willi Boskovsky

(P) 1978*

MAX REGER (1873–1916)

A Ballet Suite, Op. 130

5   *No. 1 Entrée*.................................. 3:01
6   *No. 2 Colombine*........................... 3:30
7   *No. 3 Harlequin* 2:11
8   *No. 4 Pierrot and Pierrette* 3:37
9   *No. 5 Valse d'amour* 2:52
10 *No. 6 Finale Presto*......................... 2:42

Staatskapelle Berlin

Otmar Suitner

(P) 1972*

FELIX MENDELSSOHN BARTHOLDY
(1809–1847)

A Midsummer Night's Dream, Op. 61

11 *Scherzo (Allegro vivace)* 4:31

Staatskapelle Berlin

Günther Herbig

(P) 1977*

FRANZ SCHUBERT (1797–1828)

Rosamunde, Op. 26 D. 797

12 *Ballet music No. 2*........................... 6:28

Staatskapelle Dresden

Willi Boskovsky

(P) 1978*

ANTONIN DVORAK (1814–1904)

Symphony No. 8 in G major, Op. 88

13 *Allegretto grazioso*........................... 6:34

Staatskapelle Dresden

Herbert Blomstedt

(P) 1976*

CARL MARIA VON WEBER
(1786–1826)

1   *An Invitation to the Dance, Op. 65*... 9:08

Großes Orchester des Deutschlandsenders
Robert Hanell

(P) 1972*

JOHANN STRAUSS (1825–1899)

2   *Voices of Spring, Op. 410*................. 7:07

Sylvia Geszty, soprano
Dresdner Philharmonie
Heinz Rögner

(P) 1982*

PETER ILYICH TCHAIKOVSKY
(1840–1893)

3   *Waltz of the Flowers
(from The Nutcracker)* 7:07

Rundfunk-Sinfonie-Orchester Berlin
Heinz Rögner

(P) 1982*

JOHANN STRAUSS (1825–1899)

4   *The Blue Danube, Op. 314*............. 10:13

Staatskapelle Dresden
Otmar Suitner

(P) 1981*

JEAN SIBELIUS (1865–1957)

5   *Valse triste, Op. 44 (Sad Waltz)* 4:56

Dresdner Philharmonie
Heinz Bongartz

(P) 1971*

ARAM KHACHATURIAN
(1903–1978)

6   *Waltz (from Masquerade)*................. 3:26

Dresdner Philharmonie
Herbert Kegel

(P) 1971*

ALEXANDER GLASUNOW
(1865–1936)

7   *Concert Waltz, Op. 47*...................... 8:18

Großes Orchester des Deutschlandsenders
Robert Hanell

(P) 1971*

MAURICE RAVEL (1875–1937)

8   *La Valse (The Waltz)*...................... 13:56

Berliner Sinfonie-Orchester
Günther Herbig

(P) 1979*

* VEB Deutsche Schallplatten Berlin

This compilation (P) 2005 edel CLASSICS GmbH

All Photographs by DAVID HAMILTON

Text by CHARLES MURLAND

Special thanks to the dancers at the:

THE ROYAL BALLET

MAURICE BEJART'S BALLET OF THE XXTH CENTURY

THE BOLSHOI BALLET COMPANY

THE VIENNA STATE OPERA BALLET COMPANY

PARIS OPERA BALLET

LINCOLN CENTER

and students from

London, Vienna, Stockholm, Copenhagen, Geneva and New York.

Young dancers depicted on pages 70–89
are from the DAVID HAMILTON films »Bilitis« and »Laura« available on video.

SNOW

BY HARRIET BRUNDLE

Weather
Explorers

Weather
Explorers

©2016
Book Life
King's Lynn
Norfolk
PE30 4LS

ISBN: 978-1-910512-74-6

Written by:
Harriet Brundle
Edited by:
Gemma McMullen
Designed by:
Drue Rintoul

A catalogue record for this book
is available from the British Library.

CONTENTS

Words in **bold** can be found
in the glossary on page 24.

SNOW

When the weather is very cold, sometimes it snows.

SNOW IS VERY COLD TO TOUCH!

If it is cold enough, the snow will stay on the ground.

5

HOW IS SNOW MADE?

Snow is made from water that has frozen in the sky and turned into ice.

WATER MUST BE AT 0 **degrees** IN TEMPERATURE TO FREEZE.

The ice falls from the sky in snowflakes.
When this happens, it is snowing!

SNOWFLAKE

SEASONS OF THE YEAR

There are four seasons in a year.

SPRING

SUMMER

WINTER

AUTUMN

8

The winter months are December, January and February.

SNOW IN WINTER

It is most likely to snow in the winter because it is the coldest season.

There are less hours of sunshine in winter than in any other season.

WHAT DO WE WEAR IN THE SNOW?

Snow is very cold so we need to stay warm. We wear gloves to keep our hands warm.

GLOVES

Snow boots keep our feet warm and stop them from getting wet.

PLANTS

Many plants cannot live in the cold snow.
They die in the Winter.

We can plant **bulbs** in the garden in the winter.
They will start to grow when the weather gets warmer.

BULB

15

ANIMALS

When the weather is cold, some animals will hibernate. This means they find a safe place and sleep through the winter.

Some animals live in places where there is snow all the time. Polar bears have lots of fur on their bodies to keep them warm.

POLAR BEAR

MELTING SNOW

When the sun shines on snow,
it gets warm and melts.

When snow melts it turns back into liquid water. Some of the water goes into the ground and some stays on the **surface**.

THINGS TO DO IN THE SNOW

We can make a snowman in the garden!

DON'T FORGET TO ADD HIS EYES, NOSE AND MOUTH!

It is fun to go sledging down hills in the slippery snow.

DID YOU KNOW?

ANTARCTICA

Antarctica is the coldest place on planet Earth.
It is always snowy in Antarctica.

22

Snow falls in snowflakes. Each snowflake looks different to the next.

THERE ARE NEVER TWO THAT LOOK EXACTLY THE SAME.

23

GLOSSARY

Antarctica: part of the planet on which there is always snow.

Bulb: the part that plants grow from.

Degrees: the unit we use to measure the temperature.

Surface: the top or outer part of something.

INDEX

Cold: 4, 5, 10, 12, 14, 16, 22.
Warm: 12, 13, 15, 17, 18.
Water: 6, 19.
Winter: 8, 9, 10, 11, 14, 15, 16.

CREDITS